Cleil's Trilogy
A Mother's Whimsical Genealogy
& Poetry Anthology

by
Cleil Turkington

Foreword by Lori Carangelo

Access Press

c. 1999 by Cleil Turkington
Revised and Edited 2019, by Lori Carangelo, Editor-Publisher
published by Access Press in paperback and e-book editions

previous publication
1999 by Access Press, Palm Desert, CA, as an e-book edition
ISBN 0-942605-14-4

Cover Photo: Cleil Turkington, by permission of Robert Turkington
Cover Design: Access Press

ISBN: 978-0-942605-14-3

Please accept this little book,
Remember as you read it through,
Forever you are part of me
And I am part of you.

Love,

Cleil

c o n t e n t s

BOOK TWO: CHESTER DIARY - 93

FOREWORD

CLEIL'S TRILOGY was published after Cleil's death in 1999 by permission of her children. At age 87, Cleil Turkington, mother of four, received her BA degree and began teaching, missing out on neither life nor family.

In this collection, Cleil shares her spiritual and humorous view of her ancestors, her pregnancies, her children, and her widowhood spent communing with Mother Nature together with her English bulldog, "Yo." Many of the verses were inspired by Cleil's more serene time in Chester, in Northern California.

Enjoy!

THE PUBLISHER

Book One -
Creation: A Trilogy

#1 GENESIS ONE

God said, "Let there be light"
And ever-earth was all aglow.
"Let there be life," and life was there,
No need for seed to grow.
"Let there be man-"
and there was man
All perfect in his father's plan.
By Spirit formed, of Spirit born
On that forever present morn.

#2 GENESIS TWO
THE GARDEN OF EDEN

A mist arose and watered all the earth,
And from the soil a man was given birth.
ADAM!

And he felt so much alone
That willingly he parted with a bone.
And from that bone was formed -- would you believe -
EVE!

One fateful day as Eve went for a walk
A wily snake set up some casual talk.
"I guess you know, to eat from this one tree
Is to be wise as God, immediately."
And Eve responded, "God! and just one bite?"
"RIGHT"

Eve shared with Adam. Innocence took flight.
They now stood naked in each other's sight.
And Adam said, "We need must find a tree
With ample leaves to hide our nudity.
For when God comes, he must not find us so." OH?

But when God saw what they had been about
He had one word for both. The word was "OUT!"
So toil was born that distant day
And now We live by virtue of a sweated brow.
I-low sad for us that Eve did not know "NO!"

#3 EVOLUTION

And then came Darwin and his revolution,
"Forget the Bible myths, think evolution!"
From simple cells that clumped in ancient sea

Rose myriad forms of great complexity.
The tree-of-life branched in its upward climb
And man-like creatures came all in good time.
(Could be perhaps a missing link or two.
The Theory, though, is absolutely true!)"

But rage of life continues on its way,
Don't think it stops with man as seen today.
So, shall we pause while we are still ascending,
Perhaps it time to contemplate -TRANSCENDING!

Truly it will be.
When I promised to give a short, succinct family history,
I little knew the pit-falls and a pleasure, but FUN!!!? No way!

JONES

We shall, as a matter of principle, begin with Clan Jones... (or Clan John if you will), 1782 places James Jones in Virginia, but it would appear his stay was brief, as he headed -almost at once toward the Highway 66 of the period, the Cumberland Gap. Family history places him in Tennessee.

His descendants never lost this way of referring to their parents as PAW and MAW, as the case might be, which seals him as a son of Appalachia. We see Permelia Sarles in the family now and they are in Indiana where James died. Our family historian for Jones, Joanne Jones-Lahvic, (daughter of Merrill Edwin Jones,) found the record of the auction held in Indiana. She found it very poignant, the list of auctioned articles included things such as washtubs, farm implements and one pet deer.

The name LIVELY now enters the picture--a son-in-law. James is buried in Indiana. Parmelia continued on and we last see her in Ottumwa Iowa. It appears that she and her daughter, Palina Lively, stayed there for the duration of their lives, we assume she is buried there, but the head of the family continued on to Knoxville, Marion County, Iowa. Iowa was still Indian territory at that time.

Jonathon had already married while in Indiana.
His wife, Margaret, died there.

They had two sons, one Alonzo.
Alonzo died from being kicked in the head by a horse.

Jonathon married again and his wife this time was Margaret
Merrill. Her home was Champlain, Illinois. Jonathon has the
distinction of having been the second elected sheriff of Marion
County, Iowa. (I admit to a thrill when I saw his signature on the
records of Iowa.) They arrived in Iowa approximately (this is
recorded, but I forgot,) in 1848. He was elected Sheriff in 1850, and
in 1852. Poor grandmother Margaret was the jailer, and her home
was the jail. (This may have affected her social standing.) Much
later in 1890, during the Chicago worlds Fair, Grandpaw and
Grandmaw Jones were hosting two ladies from Iowa (Agnes and
Nora White). During the night a burglar broke in. Alas, Grandpa
Jones slept in the raw and his gun was on the old square piano in
the living room. (Daughter Melissa was a music teacher.)
The burglar escaped due to Jonathon's innate modesty.

Jonathon had two sons that I know of. One, William, took off for the West and we have no other facts about him.
The second son was Thomas.
Jonathon died in Knoxville about 1906, and like Margaret Merrill Jones, is buried in the Pioneer Section of Graceland.
It is now called City Cemetery.

Thomas Carrie Ruth Andrew, about 1867. Thomas was injured in an railroad accident years before, and was a Morphine addict, as a result of the medicine of that time. Morphine was noted as the cause of his death some 40 years later. This was typical of the times. He is buried in the Union Ridge Cemetery, Cook County, Illinois.

The Andrew family helped settle the two counties of Highland and Ross, Ohio. The Census places them there around 1830. Ross is a highland clan of Scotland. The Andrew family is a sect of the Ross clan, which is something to think about when buying your tartan.

James Andrew married Delila Acton. The Actons lived in the neighboring county. Delila was English--Those of you who have traveled by bus from Heathrow Airport to London have all passed through Acton town. When Joanne was researching James and Delila, she found their marriage application--another thrill (This record is in Hillsboro, Ohio, home state of the Andrew and Actons). James and Delila left by wagon from Concord, Ohio. They arrived in Marion County close to what is now Harvey, Iowa. There they quickly found a more permanent home, Concord. They died of Cholera 2 weeks apart, and are early settlers of Concord Cemetery.

Ruth Andrew, an infant at this time, was raised by Harriet Andrew Robuck. The Robuck and Andrew families traveled together from Ohio to Iowa. Ruth and Tom Jones married in Knoxville in 1864.

Ruth, our great-grandmother where I am concerned, had five children. Grandmother Ruth had a real flair for names. Her eldest, Edwin Forest Jones, born 1865, caused real strife in the family. Tom (grandfather, should I say Grandpaw Jones) wanted him to be named for his hero, John Wilkes Booth (also an actor.)

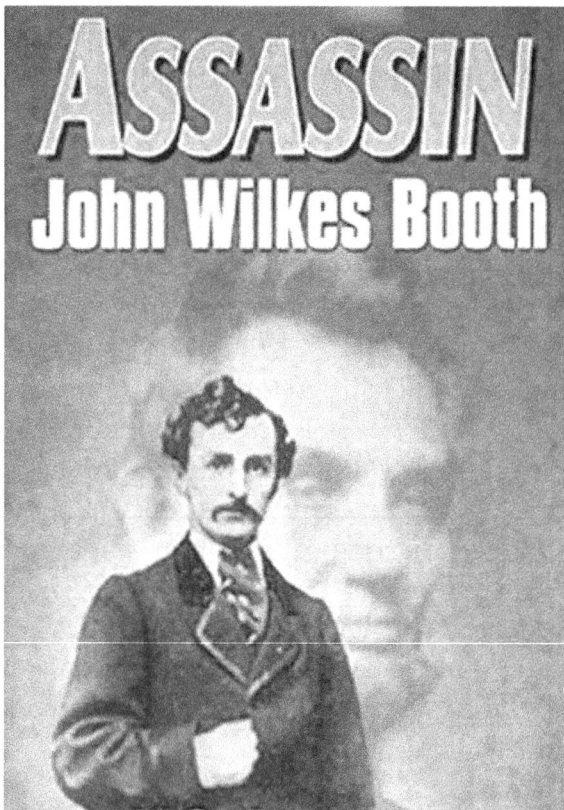

ASSASSIN
John Wilkes Booth

The second son was named Roscoe Conklin, after a popular statesman of his day. As he grew up, he did not care for his name either, and answered only to Chris. Uncle Chris was murdered in a small Knoxville hotel about 1916. His killer was sentenced to Fort Madison prison.
Oddly enough, I met his niece at a dance at Northwestern University many years later. No great friendship developed.

The next son, Jonathon Emmet, was again non-enthusiastic about his name, and as a child called himself "Don" and as an adult moved to Omaha, Nebraska, and assumed his middle name Emmet. He is buried in Omaha.
Ruth had one more child, a daughter born three days after Christmas.
It is a sad story.

The Sheriff had moved back to Chicago some years before and at the time of Ruth's death, Tom was living with him in Chicago. (When winter came and money was tight, the men would go to Chicago and find work in the stockyards.) My father was alone on the farm with Ruth and the smaller children (two daughters had swelled the ranks). I guess my father was about 16 and the death of his mother and infant daughter and the entire responsibility was on him.
He never forgave his father for being in Chicago at the time. It made him very bitter against his father. Unfairly, I think, but it must have been a terribly bitter time in their lives.

Ruth (who, by the way, was a red-haired Scotswoman) is buried in Knoxville cemetery with Chris, Edwin, Margaret and the newborn baby.)

The two girls, Mary and Margaret, went to Chicago. Mary became an expatriate, moving to Canada. Margaret married Luin Hough, who was very interested in photography and served at the University of Chicago many years, both as a photographer in the hospital, and as a textbook illustrator in the geology field. Their son, Dr. John Wesley Hough, taught both at the university of Illinois and the University of Michigan, plus special stints in India and the Antarctic. Jack married the daughter of Professor Carlson, of the University of Chicago.

EDWIN FOREST JONES

"You've made that pup a small tin god!"
My mind's ear catches father's roar.
BUT dad, before you criticize
Sit tight and let us analyze
You're dealing with amour.

I've made my pup a small tin god"
You're quite correct on THAT score
but certainly you realize capacity to idolize
Enriches ME the more.

I've made my pup a small tin god
That means I love him LOTS, therefore
I trust in YOU to emphasize
You cannot help but realize
LOVE is my tin-god's core!

CLEIL

A daughter, Cleil, and half-brother, Merrill,
completed the children of James Jones –
James to Jonathon to Tom to Edwin to Merrill.
Merrill had three daughters; Joanne, who is our historian, also
Marilyn, Cleil and the youngest, Dora Marie.
Edwin's wife, Marie Samelius, is still living in Des Plains (1992),
Illinois; with Joanne and Dora living close by.
Merrill closed the book, so far as we know, on the descendants of
James Jones--so we have a neat little package -
Merrill was talented musically; his military career was a musical
one.
After all this, we have a finally reached Cleil (WHEW)
and another family to cope with.

The Mayflower & the Pilgrim Fathers

ROMBERGERS

The Rombergers were reported to be in the new world
prior to the Pilgrims. There are many Romberger stories;
a Romberger may have paid part of the bribe
to have the Captain of the Mayflower
land in Massachusetts instead of Virginia.
It is also reported that Rombergers may have been slavers.

My mother was Edna Myrtle Romberger, born in Kansas.
Her mother, Catherine Elizabeth Crossly Romberger, was a
Quaker, born in or around Harrisburg, Pennsylvania.
They tell a tale which I do not vouch for, but as a tale that has lived
for 200 years, I shall not be the one to break the chain.

As a family of immigrants, the Rombergers, traveling to another
part of the state, stopped at an inn for the night. They ate some
kind of unfamiliar meat (which they did not care for), then
proceeded up to their unheated room. Midwinter--no fire, they
went fearful to bed--they distrusted their hosts. Restless, the leader
of the party began to investigate around--I think snooping might be
the proper word--and discovered under the bed the frozen body of
a mutilated man; the mutilation being a sizable piece of flesh had
been cut away--rump steak? They climbed out the window and
headed to another part of the state--fast. I told you I would tell it,
not vouch for it.

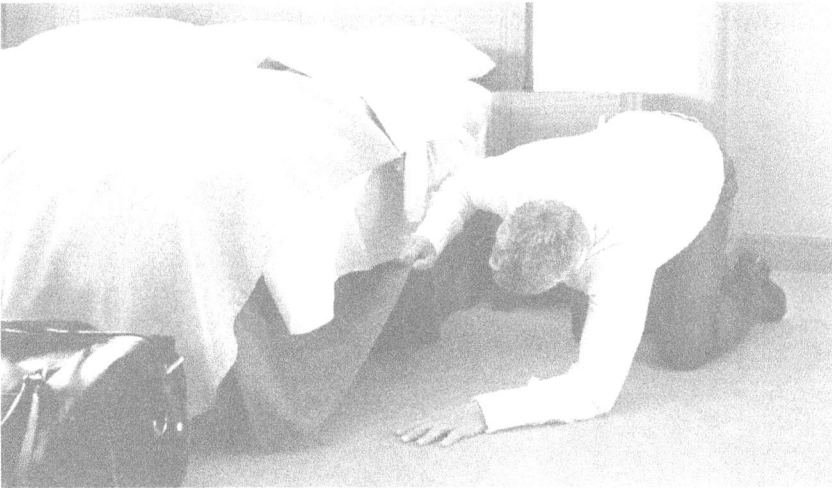

In Indian times, an Indian arrow flashed through the window and struck one of the Dutch maidens. Ever since, at irregular intervals, a black-eyed, black- haired child is born to the Romberger family. I suspect artificial insemination--here I give living proof. Aunt Eva Romberger had the coal black eyes and hair. She also told both tales (and if any of her children see this,I shall have to leave town, Pronto). I have been a bit rough on the Rombergers. Let me make amends by reporting they arrived the New World on the Good Ship Anne, quite awhile before there was much history. Valid Question: Do Rombergers belong in the group known as the Black Dutch? Certain mental and physical characteristics would imply it. The only picture of a Romberger, Christian Romberger, (born around 1790), is of a man about 70 years of age (an old tintype, probably). He looks Indian, and it justifies the arrow story; early fraternization? The Eisenhowers and Rombergers were friends and made the trip from Pennsylvania to Kansas by the Atchinson, Topeka and the Santa Fe. A little later the Eisenhowers and the Rombergers intermarried, so we have a link to President Eisenhower. These statements are verifiable, so we DO have a couple of footholds in U.S. history.

TURKINGTON

Now the Turkingtons, and we start with Mrs. W.W. Turkington, Sr,
born Clara Henrietta Anna Louise,
(at this point in time, if your initials spelled a work
you were guaranteed financial success.

Her Father was Herman Kaage (cog-e) who was born in
Luxembourg. Her mother, Louise Wreden, was born in Berlin.
Both families immigrated to Chicago,
but William Turkington did not meet Clara until in their twenties.
Clara, called Clar-kin, was the 13th child;
Both parents died while Clara was little more than a teenager
and she was raised by her sisters, Emily and Annie.

Before that, Clara's father ran a saloon,
(a fact which always embarrassed Clara in later years).
Her father also had an old wise horse,
and "Toots" (as Clara was known in our family- the name which
stuck was endowed by a sailor as he hoisted her upon a boat,
during a tour on Navy day, long since past),
used to tell how, after closing hours,
Herman would bring the horse into the saloon
and treat the animal to a foaming schooner of beer.

Bill, (William Warren Turkington I) was born September 23rd.
Toots was born October 12th.
They were born only three blocks apart.
They met, married in Stevensville, Michigan,
where Sabra Balcom lived.
Sabra was the widow of David Turkington,
who was the son of John Charles Turkington;
David and John Charles' two sisters were Anna and Sadie.

Years later, Edna Romberger Jones married John Charles
Turkington, and became stepmother to Dorothy, Lois, and John
Charles Jr.
This made Cleil Jones Turkington niece to her own mother, and
Clara Kaage Turkington and Edna Romberger Jones Turkington
sisters-in-law.
As Mike (William Warren Turkington III) so aptly expressed it,
with our Grandfathers being brothers,
it explains why this part of the family were all nuts."
Bill was very proud of the fact that in the early years he had
worked as a back stage person in Vaudeville.

Now we must skip some 55 years to
Toots, in the California Lutheran Hospital, terminal.
On Saturday morning, alone in his Pasadena apartment,
Bill is called by another neighbor—an elderly lady who had fallen
and could not rise. Bill tried to help; perhaps a heart attack, but Bill
was now prostrated. An ambulance was called, and he was rushed
to the Pasadena Hospital. Warren was called, and he called Dr
Riccardi, Bill's friend and physician. They met at the Pasadena
Hospital, and Bill was moved at once to the Lincoln Hospital.

On the way to visit Toots, Warren and I stopped first at Lincoln to
see Bill. He looked pretty shaky, so we stayed only minutes,
promising to return after visiting Toots.
Of course, we never did, as he died minutes after we left him.

Because the wedding anniversary of Toots and Bill would be
Wednesday, Toots decided to have his funeral Tuesday.
As she was not permitted to leave the hospital, I stayed with her.
I read the 91st Psalm to her, and she went to sleep not waking until
friends came in after the services; that was a blessing indeed.

The next day was the anniversary. Bill had ordered the customary
one dozen red roses prior to the incidents of Sat-ur-day!
They arrived on the day of their anniversary!

Toots, far from being upset, said calmly,
"He never forgot them before, why would he forget them this
time?" Why indeed. But I think that is the final act of a lovely tale.
To the-end they were in love, certainly if anyone was.
Born a few blocks apart, died a few weeks and a short distance
apart, with their anniversaries always observed right on schedule.

The Turkington family story is told by Mrs. Cromwell Stacy
(May Stacy, Bill, cousin) in a letter to Mickey.
This is a story told to a Grandmother by a Grandmother
concerning a mutual relative.
It again is unsubstantiated other than that the basic tale
is English History.

Facts are, Charles the 2nd had more than a casual relationship with the House of Orange (English), and he also had a generous habit of rewarding his favorites with estates in the Dublin area of Ireland.

The story:
(and the letters in the possession of Cleil Turkington Clark)
is that Lady Mary Currie, a Lady-in-waiting in the House of Orange, married a commoner, David Turkington,
and so was no longer accorded court status.
However, as an immediate-result of this marriage, David Turkington was awarded estates in Belfast, Ireland, and became an Irish Land Lord.
There was also some Canadian property, Goodrich, Canada, involved. The Turkingtons went to Canada, complete with jewels and horses.

There was a period of commuting.
Children were born and died aboard ship.
Sometimes they went through New York,
sometimes through Chicago.
It is stated that they owned considerable property
around the area of Wall street, at that time.

Lady Mary never ceased grieving for her former lifestyle.
I do not know whether death caught up with her in the new world or the old. What we do know is that the Turkingtons lived on, in Charles, John, and David.
End of the story.

In the course of time, Toots and Bill had two sons, W. W. Jr. and the younger son, James John Harold Turkington.

Because this entire book will be devoted to the children, grandchildren and great-grandchildren of W., we shall bypass him for a while and devote ourselves to the younger brother.

James John Harold was a graduate of the University of Arkansas. He had a few bad years, dogged by a Health problems while an undergrad. In due time, he rejoined the world and went south to work--thermodynamics safely behind him.

He was associated with a Southern telephone company. He married Emily Mitchell, a University of Georgia graduate. They later settled down in Birmingham, Alabama.

Their daughter, Sarah Louise Turkington, was born in Georgia. Sally, for Sarah; Louise for both great-grandmother Louise and, grandmother Clara Louise.
Sally is currently an Assistant Professor of Special Education at the University of Montevalle, Alabama.
Sally married her high school sweetheart, Gary Smith.

They have two sons, Brian Wayne Smith, a student at Shelby Academy near Montevalle. Having been accepted in special classes that permit attending college courses between senior and junior years of high school, he is enjoying archeology classes at the University.

A younger brother, Kevin, is also attending Shelby Academy, but to date he is majoring in soccer, basketball, and band.
Both seem to have a good idea of which way they wish to go.
Bill and Clara and Edna and John are all buried in Altadena, California.

WARREN AND CLEIL

And now fasten your seat belts--we enter the house of Warren and
Cleil. Most of their exploits will be in the rhymed section.
We proceed ' with caution.

Warren and Cleil, acquainted since 8th grade,
at which time Warren was 8th grade president, Master Builder,
soon to be active in ROTC at Schurz High School.
(I cannot let the ROTC go unnoticed.)
Any high school kid who could successfully roll puttees five days a
week requires special mention--I am offering it NOW.
I transferred to Schurz High School.

I founded the Biology Club and was active in Press Club.
A verse I had written for the Schurzone was printed
in the Chicago Daily News (OH BOY).
After school, Warren had a job delivering the Chicago Daily News
in a 50 mile rural route. Can I roll newspapers!
Next came graduation, 1927. Warren went on to college.
I went to work. Then came a hectic period.
My very dearest friend since the 3rd grade, died.
I got married, (Warren of course), and my father died.

We left the family home for an apartment.
I got pregnant (not for the last time).
The Depression descended,
Finally, I took the Los Angeles City Schools Teachers exam, and
went to work starting at the age of 50. And that's it. Yes I enjoyed
the experience, then retired at the age of 65.

Lest I forget, we brought Mickey, Mike and the families first bull dog (Snooty) along. Warren went back to school, and, well subsidized by Toots and Bill, life went on. Warren got his CPA and founded Los Angeles County School Claims, became Deputy County Auditor, left the county to become a Credit Union manager. Two years later, he died, just 3 days before his 71st birthday. He is buried with all the Joneses in the Pioneer section of Graceland (Knoxville, Iowa.)
Me? Back to school - 200 units, including a BA in English at age 87. Pregnancy Diary accepted by a college publication - Got two credentials.

Chester woman returns to college at age of 87

PHONE CALL

Each Monday night I have to leave
my sons and heirs alone.
They have but one requirement,
At nine I have to phone.

I dash to Student Union and
I drop my noisy dime.
The number rings and rings and rings
It seems the longest time.

Till finally there's a breathless
"Hi Boy, you should see this show.
Clark Kent's in heaps of trouble now.
Those crooks won't let him go!"

"But just you wait, he'll fix them yet.
They don't know he's the guy,"
That changes into Superman.
"Yipes, there he goes. Good-bye."

Responsively, I say "Good-bye."
(But only to a buzz.) -
Oh, well, I guess I've gained as much
As any parent does.

THANKS ROBERT!
I BRUISE EASILY!

As Mrs. T. scrambled for fossils and fun
She managed a tumble fantastic.
She hit the Jurasic
Slid through the Triassic
The very next target, or course,
her own assic.
And lacking the sturdy right arm of her son

BLACK CAMEL PATROL

Their fezzes jauntily askew
Their cumberbunds just right,
Their swagger sticks so proudly poised
--They've just marched out of sight.
In memory we'll ever hear
Their foot-falls Left and Right
OUR SHRINERS, Ever marching on
In fellowship of light.
So mote it be.
Edwin Forest Jones, Medina Temple,
Chicago
William W. Turkington, Al Malika Temple,
Los Angeles
W. Warren Turkington, Al Malika Temple,
Los Angeles

MICKEY

Our #1 child was Mickey. Her career was 100%
NON-scholastic.
Mick, not scholastically inclined,
Her mind will ever turn
Not for self but others,
To compassion, care, concern

ADVENTURES OF MICKEY

Once I had a daughter
With a one-track mind
There was just no question
SOMEDAY she would find--
Her very own Scout Master

Hanson Dam the Camp Site
She joined a Boy Scout troop.
Boating, hiking, singing,
What a gung-ho group--
And what a Scout Master!

Came the time for swimming,
And her luck ran out.
Soaking wet they noticed,
She was a GIRL scout!!

How shocked the Scout Master!
Scouts are ever ready,
Scouts are quick to think.
Promptly was grabbed
and dumped into the drink–

Who laughed? The Scout Master.
And this ends our saga, Mickey got her man
Possibly the method did not fit her plan--
BUT SHE GOT HER SCOUT MASTER!!!

MANUEL "LITTLE JESUS"- JOHN JOSEPH RENDON

I carried flowers to your grave today.
Close by, black shrouded women
knelt to pray. My lips were dumb.
I raised my heart
and once again you flew.
Your plane so high
it seemed to breach the blue.
You dipped your wings.
From heaven garnered,
benediction came
"The wind strews ash,
but God accepts the flame."
And all was well.
(Buried in Calvary, Los Angeles)

MIKE

#2 was Mike (W. W. Turkington III).
His graduations were numerous
but the only one I was able to attend was at Quantico, Virginia.
As a Lieutenant Commander, he was privileged to be part of a class
composed of officers of equivalent rank from all over the world.
Graduation saw each wearing the dress uniforms of their own
country. As long as I was only to see one graduation,
I am glad it was that one.
Following 3 deployments to Antarctica,
Mike suffered a head accident and amnesia,
and was given medical retirement.
He returned to school, took his degree in law,
and is currently Deputy District Attorney
in Mariposa, California.

LIFE WITH MIKE

Whistler patterned "Mother."
As a lady old and gray.
Lacy-capped who rocked and pondered
On a vanished day.

"Mother" now means glamour girl
Pert, vivacious, gay
Be it golf or skiing she is
Always set to play.

I am at an awkward age
But I'm a mother too
I don't "rock" nor ski but
Here's the sort of thing I do —

Head beneath the dashboard
And posterior in view.
I'm the flashlight wielder till
Transmission bolts come through.

Lacy caps don't crown my locks,
My cheeks will shame no rose.
Motherhood's one badge is just
The grease that tips my nose.

That I rate the title, though,
Each one who sees me knows,
Mothers, only mothers, could
ooze love in such a pose!

COULD THIS BE A FORECAST?
MIKE'S KITE

My tiny kite tugs at its string
Like some sky-giant at its mast,
Who, having sailed through earth's blue sky
Chafes now at being safe and fast.
Now if this string I hold so close
Should break, or slip from out my hands
My kite, like some wee vagrant ship
Would seek a port in foreign lands.

A TRIP DOWN
THE MILKY WAY (1949)

We planned a special festive board
To meet the girl our son adored.
The plastic tablecloth shone bright-
The cutlery displayed, just right.

While Tom and Rob were pledged to be
Small models of propriety.
We sat down, dressed in Sunday-best
And beamed upon our pretty guest.

I smiled, "Let's eat. Please go ahead.
Now Joan, Pleases try some fresh, hot bread."
Mike tried to serve the winsome lass.
His efforts spilled a milk-filled glass.

All leaped to help-two glasses more
Cascaded milk on guest and floor.
Then somehow Tom and Rob came through
And spilled a little water, too.

Our festive board, a sorry sight.
our well-dressed sons, a soggy fright.
Our guest, a bit the worse for wear.
And Mike, by now too numb to care.

When asked, "Where we met Joan?" We say....
"We mopped her up on the milky way!"

ROBERT

Robert (#3), is a "duck," University of Oregon,
and owns a business dealing in hazardous chemicals.
He teaches classes at universities,
pretty well all over the United States
and has taught in both Alaska and Canada.

Robert married Celinda David.
They were married in the University Chapel at Lexington,
Kentucky. They took ship at once for Australia and celebrated
their first anniversary (nine months to the day)
with the arrival of Greggory McPatrick Turkington,
a genuine Aussie.
Gregg was named for Robert's high school friend, Gregg Huser.
Richard K. McAfoos, (who was in the Navy with Robert, on the
USS Bennington, CVS 20, an Aircraft carrier, which is presently in
mothballs), and Patrick, Celinda's cousin.
The wedding was partly performed by Celinda's uncle
who is a Bishop in the Episcopal church.

Their second child, Gwynne Margaret,
is currently very active in animal rights work.
She lives in Santa Barbara, California.
Gregg is presently working with his father
at Haztech Systems, Inc.

[Editor's Note: In his later years, Robert married Rosanne, retired,
had a quadruple heart bypass, and at this writing
is enjoying his grandchildren]

Robert and Rosanne Turkington

BOBBY PAUL

Name-sake of two youthful U.S. sailors,
"Chickiell was the toddler's joy and pride.
Paul returned to proudly dub him "SAILOR."
But, a Kamakaze victim,
Bobby Paul died.
Bobby is buried in the PUNCH BOWL.
His ship was the Destroyer, Hazelwood.
*Chickie was the eagle on Paul's uniform.

FIRST CAMP FOR
ROBERT

I patted his cap
and I straightened his tie
And I just couldn't banish the pride from my eye.
As I waved a farewell
to my well-polished scamp
(WHO WILL LOOK SUCH A MESS
WHEN HE DRAGS BACK FROM CAMP)

TOM

Tom, #4, is a policeman in Paradise, California.
His life is entirely in cars.
He took the Los Angeles auto-shop,
aware of the year when he graduated from high school,
and my honest opinion is that he should have opened
a police car garage!
He took his Bachelor in Police Science
at Los Angeles State College.

What I have neglected to say to this point
could easily have me cut right off of the family tree!
Tom married Mary Pearson.
Both Tom and Mary are Angeles State University Graduates,
in Police Science.
They have two children.
Tom is a member of the Air Force,
stationed in Denver Colorado.
He is the proud owner of the bronze medal
for the Air Force Ski team.

His wife is an Air Force Brat, Renee ---
I venture to say the future of the Air Force is in good hands.
Tom's daughter, Jamie, is presently attending Chico State
University.
Jamie was named for a Police partner, one of three partners Tom
lost while a Sergeant for the San Diego Police Department.
That caused him to seek employment in a smaller Police
Department.
Chester was, I believe, a very intelligent decision.

BRIGHTEN THE CORNER (TOM)

A character garden had bubbled and bloomed. Every shining-
faced Sunday school laddy and lass
Had been given some virtue to proudly display- oh the teacher was
pleased with her class!
She had beamed upon "Honesty, Courage and Faith" But that
"Patience" had tried her she could not deny.
For my offspring had topped his most cherubic smile
With a truly impressive black eye!

POUFF !!!!

Tommy is my pride and joy
A genuine hard-bouncing boy.
He's bounced wide and he's bounced far
And every bounce has left a scar.
Count the stitches on his head--
Or on his legs and arms instead.

Sixteen here, a dozen there
With eight more hidden ' in his hair--
If all dissolved, poor Tommy's fate
would be to just disintegrate!

From trikes to bikes to Harley's
From "Als" to classic cars
His wheels ever turning on
the Freeway to the stars.

The following section is a diary I kept
during my last pregnancy.

I wanted to know what went on
before I joined the family,
So I decided in advance to keep a diary so when the question was
asked... I would not be lost for an answer.
A friend submitted it to "Statement,", the publication-
It was accepted. I did not want it published and withdrew it, along
with the comments of the instructors... Sam who I shall include-
Some show great insight.

CLEIL BREAKS THE NEWS TO WARREN

Our chromosomes are linked, my mate
And now's the time to sit and wait.
As you expand with pride and joy,
I'll do the same with girl or boy.
All in good time the world shall see
Our tribute to posterity.

PHILOSOPHICAL OBSERVATION
AND EMPIRICAL RESEARCH
ON THE FETUS

Infant, moving freely
In your hidden womb-bond sea
Sheltered in the waters
That have birthed eternally
Growth your one desire
And your only goal the light
I would contend
Just to share your single sight.

PROTEST

Tadpole why won't you try to grow
with much more grace
and much less vim?
My abdominal walls grow weary
bending with your every whim.

HIDING ???

I may turn to the left,
I may twist to the right,
I may stretch on my back,
Lazily
But however I settle,
I'm soon gently nudged--
Do you think
you are hiding from me?

TADPOLE ATTENDS A
PHILOSOPHY CLASS

Tadpole, it's too plain to see
that you don't like philosophy.
But please, react as students do,
quit your kicking, just sleep through!

FAMILY NOTE:
KATHLEEN IS BORN

You gained a new niece yesterday,
This brings the score to three.
Admittedly they got here first,
But you'll still have seniority!

FASHION NOTE   (Who cares????)

Dior decrees a silhouette that's slim
and svelt and long.
To worship fashion is to grant that
this year's curves are wrong.
Poor Tadpole, you and I are "Out,"
a paradox that does appall.
our silhouettes are not approved, but
obviously are "On the ball."

MIDDLE AGE ESCAPE

My face may bear the tell-tale lines
That time and life has wrought.
But compensation still exists...
My stomach flesh is TAUT.

HOMO SAPIENS ?

I walk like a penguin, I grunt like a pig
No elephant ever has been quite so big.
A guernsey that's freshened could well envy me -
What sort of creature will this hybrid be?

IT'S DIFFICULT TO BE
SEXPLICIT!

How brightly they ask,
"Is it boy or a girl?
Well surely they are able to see
I haven't an inkling,
(in fact it's been months
since I've known for sure
which is *me*).

DANCE RECITAL

My acrobatic infant, does it occur to you
That I am growing weary of these routines you go through?
Arm movements I could cope with.
The battlements I found rough
But now you're doing tour je tes and
I have had enough.

The four times I have fallen, I really thought I'd slipped
But viewing them objectively, I now think I was trip,
So Tadpole, I've concluded,
our partnership should cease
Express yourself -- but someplace else!
Unborn, I sue for peace.

BABY SHOWER

Joanie Babe and Mickey,
both your grandmas too
Threw a "Goodies" shower,
presents just for you.
And it's hard to mention
just what you did NOT get
Tadpole, you'll personify
"What well-dressed babies WET."

AT-HOME

You ask, "Does just sitting annoy you?"
It pains me on only one score.
When I'm forced to do all my sitting AT HOME
it leaves me terrifically sore.
(Let's go! Anyplace!)

BELIEVE IT! ITS' TRUE!

We took Casey to Grandma's to visit one day.
We walked in, but luckily she was away.
Our Casey was thirsty so there on the floor,
We gave him some water, (in front of the door).
In the best bulldog fashion he lapped up his fill.

Then tipped the bowl over, as pups often will.
I reached for the mop, left the closet door wide.
Then mopped around Casey who'd not step aside.
Through the glass of the door
Mrs. Byrnes could be seen.
I called, "Stay outside
till I get this floor clean."
Her answer was vague
It was really too clear.
She did not understand, for she said,
"How nice, dear."

Casey lunged for the door and I leaped to catch "Case."
The mop handle tripped and flat on my f ace
I landed on Casey, (on YOU Tadpole, too)
We sprawled in the water, dog, mop, me and YOU!
Mrs. Byrnes looked surprised, (as she very well might).
Then brightly, "I'll just make sure - this door is tight."
She gave it a tug, the broom closet door
Went right through the glass, which rained down on the floor.
Surely things had now reached an impossible pass.
The dog, mop, you and me strewn with glass.
And then she departed, and what could I say?
To answer, "Tell Mother I called but can't stay."
We went to see Grandma. We missed her, and yet
I'm sure that's one visit she'll
NEVER FORGET!

GLAMOROUS

Tadpole you have reached the age of eight months, though.
(And all my shorts have reached the stage
where they are being worn.....BIKINI!).

IT CAN'T LAST FOREVER

My days as a Lady-in-waiting'
are numbered Deliverance is close
(and it's honestly said)
I'll be contented when you're in your cradle
And I, ON MY STOMACH,
can stretch out in bed.

LAST OFFICE CALL, WE HOPE

Last Monday we went to the Doctors.
You acted abominable.
You kicked him right in the stethoscope
(The one place you haven't kicked me!!).

THE DOCTOR SPEAKS

I asked him when I could expect you.
His answer deliberate and slow.
"When God and yourself and the baby decide,
may I be the first one to know?"

PROGNOSTICATION

The Doctor says your heart ticks off
one hundred-forty-four
Which classifies you "feminine,"
no question any more.
He says you're strong and active,
which I do not rate as news
(My abdomen's a symphony
in classic black-and-blues).
He says with smug approval that
"You're carried beautifully.
I doubt that he is intimating
You LOOK good on me.
He thinks "about the 6th of March"
should do for your debut.
But he is mute when I would know,
"Will there be curls on you?."

X-RAY

Saturday we had our picture taken
Detailed, but it lacked in dignity.
It showed you standing smack up on your noggin,
And occupying quite a bit of me.
The Doctor found it very satisfying,
The exit was both adequate and near.

He "shot" me and asserted with assurance,
"Tomorrow" this young lady will be here."
Four shots in all and they brought on a deluge,
The wettest day I've ever waded through.
But you are stubborn!!
Though today is Monday,
We co-exist as one and not as two.

SUSAN IS SPRINGTIME

New leaves and buds corsaged brown boughs
The blessed day God gave you birth.
You sought to be a part of Spring
And chose the arms of Mother Earth.
CJT, March 19, 1955

SHARE BABY

Joanie and Cleil were Ladies in waiting,
A well-rounded duo, I'm sure you'll agree.
Then fair Katalinda was born to the family
Just one lady waiting, and that one was ME!

Palm Sunday Eve and expectancy ended.
Our Susie arrived but wasn't to stay.
The spirit of Easter prevailed and she left us-
We plan on a family reunion some day.

Two Mothers, One baby.
No doubt that could end as a sad situation,
with deepest despair.
But Fair Katalinda was tucked in her bunting,
Joan brought her to me and said,
THIS ONE WE SHARE!

So fair Katalinda became my share-baby
You-think she's been spoiled a little? COULD BE!
A share child blessed with a duo of mothers
Ask who loves her most?
and the answer would be ME

From Cleil and Warren there came FOUR
From those four there came FOURTEEN
So far, from those there came SIXTEEN

THE HOUSE OF MICKEY

Carol William Margaret Michael Susan
Cameo Cody Michael Jennette Kathleen
Kery Jeremy William Britainy

WE ARE EIGHT!!!!!!!

Once Mickey had three bairns to raise,
Small Carol, Margy J. and Will.
Now Sonny had three children, too.
Young Kathy, Baby Steve and Bill.
Naturally, Mick married Sonny and
All six children had two parents.

Confusion came with "Bill" and "Will',,
So "WILL" decided, he'd be "Bob."
And life went on its hectic way.
(When THEY said family, they meant MOB)!
And though I tried, I never learned that
"Little BOB" was once our "WILL."

SIX CHILDREN!! Most of us would say
Enough! Sufficient! NOT ONE MORE!
But Mick and Sonny went their way:
And two new infants upped the score!

So now it's eight, with........
KATHY, BILLY, STEVIE, CAROL, BOBBY, MARGIE J.
Plus Mike and Susie …PHEW!!!

ZIG ZAG (with Margaret)

She honored me in Munich,
Vienna, and in Rome.
Escorted me in Sydney
Then brought me safely home.

She browned on Fiji's beaches,
Turned blue in Alpine snow.
Glowed green on Channel ferries
That whisked us to and fro,
Gulped air in Machu Pichu,
Fell flat in Iguasu
Delighted in La Boca,
OH LADY I LOVE YOU!

Asuncion, lost tourists!
(so spider-like it's planned.)
Then on to El Dorado,
OFF FOR NELSON LAND!
The outback in Australia,
(One motor quit the plane!)
New Zealand, Rocotura,
Night swimming in the rain.

Her Majesty in London,
The tower and the shows.
The stately Changing of the Guard
Which every tourist knows.

West Minster and Aunt Mary,
Paree and Perla, Chais.
The Rhine, the Rhone, the Amazon,
The Northern Lights display.

Fair Tasco, gleaming silver!
Loved Guatemala, spring.
Next modern brave Brazilia
Sheer awe for everything!

A ball at Ipanema! (It almost struck her head--
Apologies and roses! Spicy, fragrant, red.)
And off again to Venice,
Now lets give coins a toss.
But in Cologne she shivered so She rated it as "loss."

Then Erin paid a bonus,
Two new friends, "Len" and "Shirl."
Hello to Bonnie Scotland
A happy farewell whirl.
A final trip to London,
The underground ALONE !

(Then Peter at the hotel door--
She wished held used the 'phone.)
--and all of this was lots of fun
And how the time just flew.
It always seemed there were at least
A million things to do—

BUT NOW, She "does" my checkbook.
She takes me to the store.
She's driven me to service
Half dozen times or more.
It isn't too exciting,
But it's at times like this.
She has an opportunity
To dream and reminisce!.

COMMENTS OF THE CSUIA FACULTY ADVISORS

"Great in detail delightful dialogue
warm feeling of happiness
superbly expressed as flippancy.
Must have been written by a man
as no woman could be so objective."
"Good combination of humor and pathos.
Very good in parts
but the end is not characteristic of the rest.
Eliminate the last two segments."
"Until the last two segments,
this is excellent.
Provocative, well-written, humorous,
tenderly sensitive in all aspects."

MICHAEL WARREN

Now I'm on a new adventure,
Met my youthful son and heir!
MICHAEL WARREN--with that name
He's bound to meet success somewhere.
Signs imply that he'll be loyal
(At present, to each family pet--)
Sacha, Mischa, both are buddies
(Girls haven't made it yet.)

But he's gutsy, self-reliant
Goes to school without complaint
He KNOWS NO! means NO, nor argues--
still he's NOT in line for saint.
In this world, weighted with forecasts
one fact stands out vividly
I love my special Mom and Dad
and both of them love me!!

CAROL WALLACE CHRISTIAN

Today Carol's happily wed.
ONE PROBLEM; She tearfully said
"When the smoke alarm beckons
My new husband reckons
It's signaling "time to be fed."

BREAKING THE NEWS

Our chromosomes are joined, my mate. Now for nine months we'll
sit and wait To greet our precious neonate.
The egg will turn to embryo, the fetus form
and start to grow.
And so will 1! In fact, my dear,
I want to look good front, side or rear
until our precious child is here.

PROGRESS (13th week)

Hello there little tadpole in your so secret sea.
Your tiny fingers stretching out and wiggling constantly.
Those pinkish buttons on your feet
will someday turn to toes.
And see that extra special bump?
That's going to be your nose!

Just keep on growing, tadpole, please.
You've still so MUCH to do-
(But now a secret,
will you be My pinkie or boy blue?).
NO MATTER! You're OUR tadpole, OURS!
Complete those odds and ends.
You're anxiously awaited
by your-family and your friends!

TO MY MOTHER:
CAROL WALLACE CHRISTIAN

I checked the calendar today
Just four more weeks to go

And then I'll leave this tiny place
and finally meet you, face to face,
We'll both be glad I know.

I'll grasp your finger in my hand
And OH! how proud you'll be

I'll squeeze it just a little bit
(I know I'll be an instant hit!)
And then you'll cuddle me.

There's oh so much we both must learn
But we'll make out just fine
'Cause I love you, and you love me

We'll just do what comes naturally
Oh, MOM! I'm glad you're MINE!

BABY IN WAITING
SATURDAY, SEPTEMBER 10th

September ninth's ADMISSION DAY
But no, she did it her own way
(so all things soon shall go)
And so it was, the family
In best of voice sang joyously
Bienvenidos CAMEO –
WHERE WERE YOU YESTERDAY?

MY SON!

Cody my son,
all my life I have waited
and dreamed of the cherub
who'd someday be you.
But now I've quit dreaming;
you're right here.
A wonderful dream
that has somehow come true.
Your curls are flaxen,
your eyes are bright blue
Your smile rings bells,
roses spring from them.
I'll love you forever,
but please son, please,
Who in the deuce taught you how to say "No".

DADDY'S GIRL

I was warm and I was snug,
But there was something missing.
Take for instance, cuddles,
Take for instance, kissing.

Take for instance Daddy!
Where ever can he be?
I'm his precious child,
HE should be with ME!

So I sort of whimpered,
So I sort of cried.
Then I heard loud footsteps
rushing to my side.

And then HE snatched me up,
and set my heart awhirl.
Just the way it ought to be--
I AM DADDY'S GIRL.

WELL KNOWN FACT

It challenged logic,
It hints of mendacity.
But all pint-sized kids
Have full gallon capacity
(Hey! Pass me a Pamper!)

THOUGHTS FOR A THREE A.M. FEEDING

James Michael Dansie,
A brand new bouncy boy.
A brand new mother's pride,
A brand new father's joy.
James Michael Dansie
"Our Father" gave you birth.
A tempting taste of heaven,
His angel came to earth.

SURPRISE

I am Daniel Dansie.
I flew where angels feared to tread.
Just imagine the confusion--I USURPED FELICIA'S BED!

FELICIA

I am sweet Felicia Dansie,
Mine the best grin ever seen
Daddy brags about his family--MINE!
THREE ACES AND A QUEEN!
I've a feeling someone's missing (My poor mind is all awash)
Daniel--James--and THEN Felicia?
OH, MY GOSH--WHERE IS JOSH!!

OLD 69

Standing like Gibralter,
A gutsy sturdy guy,
"Rio Hondo All-league Guard--"
He lets Nobody by.
"Lets shove him over fellows--He's just a South Passpunk."
They charged as one in perfect form
AND DOWN THEY WENT KERPLUNK.
DON'T TWIST THE TIGERS TAIL
HE'LL DOWN YOU IF YOU TRY.
WE'RE THE FIGHTING TIGERS from SOUTH PASADENA
HIGH!
HOUSE OF THOMAS MERRIL
Thomas Jainie

LOU'VILLE In '92"

From "Trike" to "Bike" to "Harleys"
From "All to classic "rods"
Tom is off to Lou'ville
to challenge fortunes gods
Gumbie, born in 135
Just may not win a prize
But as he travels 66
He'll moisten many eyes
"Remember when we had one?
Those Pontiacs were tough
Just knowing that we owned one was always prize enough!

DOG DAYS

Both boys went to the dogs this year
"Cappy" Rob and his trusty gun posed for the papers
so that folks could know
"Get thee to the Dog Show for the games and fun."

DOG WEEK came and the Cover Boy
No one else but Tommy and his ready grin--
"Want to join our family?
It's no trick at all
Fall in love with any dog and MOVE RIGHT IN!"

EVOLUTION OF MAN TO BOY

Stout Hop-a-long Cassidy's riding the trail,
Determined that Justice for all shall prevail.
A brave man who never would hunt for a fight
But cowboys must always stand up for the right.
My prized copper tray's on the tournament field,
Sir Ivanhoe finds it an admirable shield,
I cringe at the blows as I hear a voice sing
"Press forward to victory for Richard, our King."
There's been an invasion of men from the stars,
(the ones wearing fish-bowls are soldiers from Mars.)
They reach middle age before they enjoy
the privilege of playing the part of a boy.

SHALL WE JOIN THE
CHILDREN? KITES!

Hills stretch tall, from the highest place
My sons toss kites to the wind's embrace.
I stand below and can plainly see
By telltale kites where my sons must be.
I call in vain and must lamely say
"The wind has carried my voice away."
The street below sounds a siren chime.
My sons appear in near-record time.
"A quarter, please, Boy! We're sure in luck,
We heard the bell of the ice-cream trucks
They're off again, while I squarely face
Twixt voice and chime,
I take second place!

SHAMPOO FOR MICKEY

When my hair is all covered
with bubbles of soap
White as snowdrifts on some winter's day,
Gentle fingers of water,
like soft April rain
Come and carry the soap-drifts away.

RELATIVE CERTAINTY

Where the cake sits on the table,
Three dark luscious layers high.
There's a big roast in the oven.
(Tweaks your nose as you pass by.)
There's a salad, jelled and sparkling
There are rolls, tidbits galore.
But depend on it, the table will be graced
by just we four.
But tomorrow, when I'm cake-less
And the rolls are day-old bread,
When the salad's just a puddle,
From which all the jell has fled.
When the roast is just the flavor,
That propels the hash along.
Then the relatives will gather,
Three full generations strong!!!!

FIRST TRIP TO LONDON AND PARIS –
THEY WENT ALONE
TOM 12, ROBERT 15 -
PARENTS, PETRIFIED

Tom and Rob are off to London.
Saturn helped them on their way.
Wistfully they left their air-steed–
Home was very far away,
Baden Powell, elite of hostels,
Fish and chips, the underground,
off to Southport and their sponsors
(Those kids really got around.)
Off to Edinborough and Blackpool
off to Dublin, (What a sea.)
Heads and stomachs still unsteady
They took off for Gay Paree.
The Metro and the Eiffel Tower The arch
and then Bastille Day Still dancing,
they enplaned on Saturn-Revoir,
but we'll be back some day--like next year,

JUST THE PLACE FOR AN ASIDE ON TRILOBITES!

Behold the fossil trilobite!
This ancient adamantine mite
Sluffed off this mortal coil we know
Five hundred million years ago, or better yet.

GOLD LACE PHILACTERY

Gold lace come naturally to some
They wear it with a flare even when it can't be seen
You somehow know it's there
Ana Maria, fell down 10 stairs backwards
probably in her gold lace **PHILACTERY!**
A SALUTE TO A FANTASTIC BRUISE

CONFESSION OF A CHRONIC CHOCOHOLIC

No drinking, no smoking,
not clever at joking,
Four letter words? G-U-T-T.
PROFANITY?
Never!
My tongue will forever Rebel at such language from me.
But still I'm a sinner,
and no mere beginner-
I've one cardinal fault to confess.
Say "CHOCOLATE,"
I stutter,
my pulse starts to Say
"CHOCOLATE",
I swoon and say
YES!
Double Dip, Please!
(Flutter)

SIMPLE FACT

Blind evolution has permanent-ized
Some cherished monstrosities hominid
that has been spared Spectacular Ischial collosities.
To get back to earth– Though changing,
still changeless eternal creation evolving,
conforming to some endless plan Emergence,
erosion and sedimentation
and total the journals of earth and man.

FRIENDS
THE LADIES GROUP

One by one sift seconds passed by
Through life's fragile hour glass.
Golden grains that filtered through
mark the moments shared with you.

MESSAGE TO MARGARET

Pain is a capering phantom.
Illusive, unreal, untrue.
It would lead us to idols of potions,
Pink pills and electric shocks too.
(Though your mind may be out like a light.)

YES, all of these pathways will lead you from pain
BUT WHERE IS THE PATH WHICH IS RIGHT?
We were formed by our Mighty Creator.
We have shuttled for 8,000 years.
We've gone forward and backward,
been stupid, or wise.
Wallowed in ecstasy, tortured in tears.

BUT On one point I'm clear,
our Creator Is kindly, benign and supreme
There are times I suspect,
all our problems add up to a self-induced dream
YEP! I think so.
So next time the capering phantom would ply me
with potions and pills
I'll sign-on with the bonafide healer, Exit to the unreal ills
At the capering phantom we'll just thumb our noses
and from this time on--life will all come up roses.

ELIZABETH'S SUNRISE SALUTE

Good Morning, Dear Father,
And thanks for this hour
In which to acknowledge
Your love and your power.
How pleasant to know that this days' course is charted.
So thanks again, Father
(WHAT SAY WE GET STARTED!)

GRACE

And after God created all
He paused and took a second look
and then proclaimed,
"JUST ONE MORE THING,
I think I'm going to write a book!
"I'll start with one and one makes two,
Expand to problems more complex
But bare in mind, I'm always there
To guide you through some weighty text.
"But quit you can't, go on you must.
One solemn promise I declare --
YOU'LL *FIND NO* PROBLEM IN MY BOOK
UNLESS THE ANSWER'S ALSO THERE-"

DONNA

DONNA THE LEPRECHAUN, LADY OF FASHION
QUICK SILVER, BUBBLE UP
LAUGHTER AND PASSION'

In his manly grip, her finger;
"How can infants be so strong!"
(Hang on, Jamie, two more years - then
Competition comes long...
You'll need that strength!)

TEENY-V

WHITE is the color of angels.
The color of Teeny-V too.
Her's is the gift of compassion,
She comforts as angels must do.
WHITE is the arc of the bright sward,
God's warrior-angel once plied.
WHITE is the bosom of Mary,
Her savior secure at her side.
WHITE is the veil of mercy
That hides the despairing from view.
WHITE is the color of angels and saints
And cherubs, and Teeny-V too.

A DAY TO REMEMBER

In the Salt Lake birthing center
just a few short hours ago.
There arrived a special infant.
Sweetest gift God can bestow.
Love surrounds him as he slumbers,
Welcoming, the family prays,
Gathered round his little cradle
On this hallowed day of days,
Heavens light is all around him
Tiny infant, God-sent quest,
Truly this a Holy family
That the love of God has blessed.

THE WADING POOL

--Madonna in a wisp of blue.
Son secure in your embrace.
Customs change, but love abides
Mothers mirror Mary's grace.

HOME SAFE!

I give you a tale of Barstow and sex
and a maid on her very first date.
The tumult which surged in her burgeoning breast
was akin to which all can relate.
He tried to seduce her with flattering words,
(Just a snake-in-the-grass, that's for sure.)
"How proud she should be to be ravished by HIM--"
(such sexplicit-ness panics the pure.)
But snakes weren't her thing, and true virtue must win.
She took-off, and soon all Barstow heard her maidenly shout,
"YOU HAVE PROBABLY MISSED--
OH JUST SKIP IT! I CAN'T USE THAT WORD."

HOUSE OF MIKE

Kathleen Scott Robin Belinda Heather James Daniel Joshua Felicia
Tawney Amber Bonn Kelsey Haley Gessylyn Casey Conner Bailey

GOD LOVES UNITED STATES SAILORS!

He never served aboard a ship?
However can it be?
Wasn't he a SAILOR
In our GREAT NAVY!

On the Carburnero
He-plowed the ocean floor
But we have it straight from him
They never "cracked" a door.

They put him in an airship
now high and dry was he
at least he had a window
and he could SEE the sea.

But Fate still held the Joker
And that was how that he
could be assigned to liaison on
A Chinese ship at sea!!!
oh this, his Chinese home
away from home he served for many a day.

BUT when they brought him back to port
it was joy to hear him say
"THIS 'HITCH' MADE ME
A SAILOR
in OUR GREAT NAVY!"

JOANIE MEETS JAMIE

Joanie went to see the baby-
"He's so cute and he's so sweet! "
Look, his fingers, pink and wiggly,
See those precious little feet.
He's so handsome! He's so macho!
See those teeth--oh-wait awhile
Right now he has other projects,
Did you'-catch that winning smile!

BELINDA TURKINGTON
BORN IN OKINAWA

Treasure of the orient
Enigmatic, sour-sweet.'
Celebrate her natal day.
Bring her buds that are most mete.
Nutmeg, pepper (That's a must)
cinnamon (A princess' price)
Bring her ginger bring her cloves;
Bring of all that makes her nice!
Titillating —
Scintillating —
Aggravating —
Belinda!!!

BIENVENIDOS, ESTRELITA!

Have you heard about the brand-new star in Texas? It is just the
brightest star there's ever been.
It is brilliant
Scintillating
sparkling
gorgeous,
And by the way, they've named it Jessalynne.
The Lone Star State now flaunts two stellar bodies.
One star for Texas, one-star for our kin.
No longer are the eyes of Texas on us,
Adoringly, they're on Jessalynne!

SOMEWHERE IN FRANCE (1979)

The bus stopped and I crossed the road.
I trespassed onto fresh-tilled land,
The farmer seemed to understand and placed a seedling in my
hand.
We smiled; it might have all been planned.
We knelt together in the row.
I tucked my seedling in just so.
He firmed it well so it would grow.
Then it was time for me to go.
We smiled "good bye". I crossed the road.
What did you do in France?
I planted lettuce.

DEAR WARREN:

Then it was so very simple.
Going to you, I would say
"Please advise on this decision -
I'd attend, then go MY way.
Now it's really not that easy
Problems bog me in-despair.
Lacking your August opinion
I just can't get ANYWHERE!
East is East, and West is that way.
Switch them and you have a mess.
Same old bind; without your NEVER
How am I to find my YES?
Love, Cleil 1983

COINCIDENCE

One by one, swift seconds pass
Down life's fragile hourglass
Golden grains that filtered through
Mark the moments shared with You.

I GIVE YOU, MR. AND MRS. DANSIE
(Heritage House, March 12, 1983)

Where else blue-bells in a cluster,
Where else men in smoky gray
Where else heart-flecked lacey ruffles?
This is Katalinda's Day.
(Where else matrons, jeloored by kisses?
Where else fathers' squiring two?
Where else bride's bouquets that clobber
Matron, first, then maiden too!)
Where else smiling, laughing, blessing,
Where else tears to sweetly bide?
Where but here in Salt Lake City
Toast the groom and kiss his bride!

AUGUST 1984

Our Katalinda's going to have a baby
She's full of pride (and full of baby, too.)
Her only problem, shall she "do" the cradle
in baby-pink or maybe baby-blue?
It matters not,
for Katalinda's certain
That God will bless her home at least once more.
And ALL she'll ask is,
Please, most Gracious father
Just send a different model than before."

THE CHANGING PHAZE OF TEXAS (1985)

Her der-ri-ere is vested with a halo.
(No bottom in her very special chair!)
Her tiny fingers dabble in warn water.
(A training aid that ended up nowhere.)
So now she roams the house, a semi-nudie.
No inhibition tells her that must stop.
NO INHIBITIONS!
Nothing says it better.
Hey Lloyd! Belinda!
Someone get a mop.
So Jessalynn is being trained with patience,
(At least they're giving it the "college" try)
But personally, I have a firm conviction
That never more shall Texas be called dry!

JUNE 10th, 1986

INTRODUCING.......I am Daniel Joseph Dansie,
Just short months go I was snuggled down in Heaven
Then it happened so-- Salt Lake City had a family
with much love to share.
I just packed my diaper bag and headed off down there.
Here I am! My parent's treasure.
I'm their pride and joy.
Brother James is happy also
Now he's dad's BIG boy.

HAPPY BIRTHDAY IKE! 1986

Ike has just turned ninety-one.
BOY! The thinest he's seen and done.
Saw the Kaiser get his pants
Ripped by bayonets in France.
Heard the birth of radio,
Saw the rise of video
Bustles went; bikinis came
Can things EVER be the same?
Front seat for the whole damned show
Didn't miss a thing, and so --
Life may find some few perplexed,
NOT IKE! His only thought, "What's next?"

I WILL CLOSE THIS VOLUME
WITH A COUPLE OF MY FAMOUS 3 A.M.-ers

I am; I was; I shall forever be.
Life-essence shuttled endlessly
Through God's Love plotted tapestry
The mountain's there for climbing
The summit still a mystery
Perhaps its time to heed
The hinted word of History,
LOVE THY NEIGHBOR !

Book Two - Chester Diary

Chester (formerly Big Meadows), in Plumas County, Northern California, is located along State Route 36 and Lake Almanor

AN INVITATION FROM CLEIL AND YO

We love our wild roses,
We love the daisies too.
In fair exchange we're giving
The cities all to you
We love our mountain river,
We love our private creek.
If you will come and visit us
We'll share whereof we speak.

SING A SONG
OF CHESTER

I know we'll always be a part of Chester.
Somewhere in that vast sweep of blazing blue
There'll be a little spot that's labeled CLEIL.
Look closely and you'll see that Yo's there too.
In Spring the meadow is an emerald island.
In Fall, the stubble turns to antique gold
And ever from capricious winds a forecast,
"This meadow soon shall shiver
white and cold."
North Fork is a rough and ready river.
Great boulders flank the rocky river bed.
Ducks bump along its ever chortling surface
And giant trees form galleries overhead.

So YO and I forever "opt" for Chester.
The fork, the wind, the meadow and the sky
Tucked in, protected by majestic mountain.
A tiny town that let the world roll by.

WE REMEMBER CHESTER - 1986

Come little wight, it is time to remember.
Our beautiful meadow is hosting the Spring.
Each sun spot cups the quiver the living
Impatient to grow -- there's a blessing to bring.
HUSH little wight, there's the moon in our meadow,
Revealing what sunlight forever has missed,
Buttons of moonbeams erupting to mushrooms
AND LOOK! 'Mere our foot prints dissolving in mist!

CLEIL'S GARDEN

I've found my niche in Life.
I share a bench with Yo
Contended we sit side by side
And watch the flowers grow!

IDYLL OF SPRING

Oh I would be a poet,
The budding Spring to cheer.
To croon in adoration,
As fragile blooms appear.
The blossom swaddled plum tree,
Azaleas, skirts awhirl,
The formal prim camellia
A Sunday-school bound girl.
The daffodil and callas
All gold and molded snow.
And up-start JOHNNY JUMP UPS
They're everywhere I go.
Oh I would be a poet,
To laud these blooms I prize.
ALAS, I am the gardener
I'M OFF TO FERTILIZE!

VIRGINIA'S GARDEN

The stirring of the sweet peas in my garden
Spills fragrance on the sparkling Springtime air.
Surrounded by God's harmony and beauty
I sensed my sainted abuelita there.
There ghost-like memories seem most at ease.
Two worlds joined, my own and abuelitas'
Infinity encompassed by sweet peas.

GARDEN OF THE TIGER

My garden sipped the summer sun,
It's posies, row on row,
Stood sentinels of day and night
Saw seasons come and go.
I bought a pup, a precious pup
Ten pounds of teeth and wag.
He made my garden his domain.
No longer may I brag.
Magnolias, children of Cathay,
Lie, whittled to the ground.
Arrogance of Spanish broom
Is nowhere to be found.
Hawaiian Gingers spicy spikes
No longer scent the air
Where once their vibrant roots sought life
A hole lies, stark and bare.
Australia's green and luscious fem
Unfurls no feather frond.
Alas! It could not tolerate immersion in the pond
My golden Holland daffodils
Which held the sun's own light
Are gone (though never quite forgot)
One bulb; one bloom; one bite!
I sing a song of garden gone.
Yet, when all's said and done
My pup is twice as precious now
He's truly "Two in one."

GARDEN, MAY 28, 1985

My garden's fantastic!
A late winter snow
Has transformed the blossoms,
A few you may know.
My iris is chic in its winter array,
Each pink stands so smart in its snowflake beret.
Shy pansies are wearing a ruffle of ice --
And violets -- there you will have to look twice.
(They're safe from the snow, snuggled under a leaf.)
One flamboyant poppy, whose debut was brief,
Just looked at the snow and then went back to bed.
"I'll just sleep it out 'til the sun comes," she said.
Intrepid as ever, quite used to hard knocks
"It's all in a day" said the snow-burdened phlox.
You've heard from the flowers (how sagely they speak)
So now hear the gardener, "I find it unique
To witness this mingling of blossoms and snow,
But I quite understand, this is Chester, you know!"

THE GARDEN OF THE LORD
(United Methodist Church, Chester, CA.)

In truth, the Garden of the Lord
Can know no blight nor setting sun.
Secure in this most sacred place
Love blossoms 'till earth's day is done.

CHESTER GOLD RUSH

Chester's wearing daffodils!
Golden bursts star emerald hills.
Roadsides glitter, garden plots
Model golden polka dots.
Daffodils in friendly knots
Dapple fields with golden spots.
Spring her golden largess spills
Chester's wearing daffodils!

ALL ABOUT BLUE

Chicken-Little spread the tale
And we thought it wasn't true
'till today when Yo and I
Walked a world flecked with blue.
In the meadow it was splattered,
By the roadside it was scattered,
Near the river it had spattered,
'Mere was just one color mattered,
Bits of blue-blue-blue.
Though the sky seemed quite intact
Chicken-Little "Told it true."
Earth had not a single nook
Lacking bright cockades of blue.
There's just no place you don't pop-out
Square-cut petals seem to crop-out
(Strewing blue-blue-blue!)

GOLDEN DAY LILY
(BEE LINE)

Chaliced in chameleon,
A dedicated bee garnered golden pollen
With stubborn industry.
Filled his little baskets And then buzzed on his way.
GIFT OF BEES! Next summer
Shall wear a bright nose-gay.

HEATHER

Heather mists the hills of Scotland.
If the legend tells it true,
Gifted with a sprig of heather
He'll be faithful who loves you!

POPPIES

Poppy buds erupt at dawn. POUFF!
Each snug green cap is gone.
Loosened petals, night-time-furled,
Wig-wag, "Have a good day world!"

POPPIES AND DREAMS

Bright did the scarlet poppies blow
In the sweet fields of long ago,
Beside the waving wheat and rye
Under the blue of summer sky.
Brightly our youthful dreams did glow
In that lost world but now we know
That poppies die when petals fade
With many dreams that once we made.
-Jean Rimmer, friend of Cleil's,
Southport, England

PURPLE DELPHINIUMS

Majesty of purple blossoms
Clustered close in vibrant spire
Crowned by golden butterflies,
Heir to vanished pomp of Tyre.

GRASS WIDOW IN CHESTER

Call her Lady Twinkle-Toes!
Everywhere she blithely goes.
Colors radiate from shoes
Vibrant with the rainbows hues.
Never path so dark and gray
Never cloudy dreary day.
But responds and even glows,
Touched by Lady Twinkle-Toes.
Colors sing, but can they chime?
Yes, I think perhaps, sometime
Listen closely as she goes
Lovely Lady Twinkle-Toes.

GARDEN WEDDING

They had a garden wedding,
Quite high society.
Two elegant delphiniums
Pledged their fidelity.
The bride in whitest splendor,
The groom in royal blue,
Joined lavender - frocked bridesmaids
And mini-maidens, too.
The priest, a doughty thistle,
Spoke with authority,
"Let no man put asunder
Those who've been joined by me!
It was a lavish wedding,
The choir one-hundred strong
(A cloud of azure chickory
Presenting LOVES SWEET SONG.)
The congregation buzzing
Like bees (of course some were)
Joined other wing-ed creatures
To happily aver.
A most delightful wedding
A highlight of the year"
(And then, o surreptitiously,
Let fall a tiny tear --
While mortal folk, like me, I
Remarked the gentle fall of

BIRD SONG

The mockingbirds in our neighborhood
Have, positively "gone Hollywood".
'They're exhibitionists, flying high
And hurling their songs at the very sky.
Responsibilities, NOT A ONE!
They hatched the eggs and then they were done.
They eased the young from the family tree -
And who does the babysitting??
ME!

ANY SPRING

List as the birdies all sing out ecstatically.
Note that earth's young are behaving erratically
Poets are working on earth-shaking sonnets
Ladies indulging in zaniest bonnets
Bunnies are bounding and chicks are all cheeping
Earth's "on the go" from her winter of sleeping
(even in Chester where snow is still snowing
bulbs as they shiver are set to get growing.)
Here in the flatlands a bee's unto stinging
NOW WE CAN SAY IT!
SPRING'S INTO SPRINGING!

SPRING WILL BE LATE THIS YEAR!
(March 17, 1989)

Today the Little Leprechauns stoned Chester
To aid in "greening-up" the waiting earth -
So many little sprouts, and shoots and seedlings
AU anxiously awaiting - Springtime birth.
ALAS! The Little Leprechauns are helpless!
Their eyes grow wide,
"How can the wee things grow?"
For what they saw --
not anxious earth "in-waiting."
But heaps and mounds
and dazzling drifts of snow!

DREAM IN THREE-D

Century participant
In nature's heedless whims.
Gnarled trunk and skyward reaching
Seed and leaf-decked limbs.
Sleeping giant, in your reverie
You dreamed of snow.

Now you've shared that vision
Fuzzy flakes float to and fro.
TREE! YOU USED THAT DREAM TO BID
YOUR RIPENED SEEDS FAREWELL!
Clouds of ghosts-of-snow engulf us.
Conjured by your spell.
We are eating, breathing, scuffing-up
Your bits of fluff.

EDUCATION OF YO

Yo found a friend on the trail today.
Far down the path I could see them at play,
Leaping and circling,
they romped and they spun,
Then YO came running from games and from fun.
Snuffling,
(he really was in quite a funk --)
Sadly enough, his new friend
was a SKUNK!

SOMNUS
IN CHESTER

My little stream meanders
Making music as it flows.
Beside our mini-river
Lithe and lovely aspen grows.
Near by darker, stalwart pines
Protect and dominate.
A tranquil setting, one in which
Yo would participate.
He has no words to praise this glade
Where magic seems "on call"
But silence! Somnus speaks --
"Soft, satisfying snores say all!"

MUCH ADO ABOUT DOING NOTHING AT ALL

What do you do on days like these?
The wind is teasing the aspen trees.
High in the sky (How high is high?)
A lazy, indolent cloud sluffs by.
Humming, the creek salutes the day.
A snake slides by in its silent way.
Yo is awake Oust one eye closed.)
And I suspect I myself have dozed.
Honor this perfect summer day --
Choose a dream and then dream away!

HOLLYHOCK

In your perky Tu-Tu,
Pollen on your nose,
Posing high upon your swaying stalk.
Pecking in my window,
"Peeping Tom" for sure.
Summer's Happy hoyden,
Hollyhock!

FALL HAS COME!

The sun had shifted to another pathway
As lazy Summer days slipped into Fall.
Today we walked the meadow near the river
Accompanied by shadows ten feet tall!!!

YO SURFS WITH THE DUCKS!

We stood on the bank,
The summer was old,
water level was low,
And ever so cold.
A tumult of sound,
A quack and a splash,
Two ducks round the bend - a down-river-dash!
Two ducks PLUS MY DOG!
Next bend hid the view.
COME BACK, YOU DUMB DOG.
THAT GAME'S NOT FOR YOU
And back came my dog.
So macho; so wet.
"Did you see those ducks?
They're wind-surfing yet.
I chased them for sure -
But then I had luck.
When water's this low
"I swim like a duck"

FISH STORY

To my little stream, exclusive,
Swam a little fish, elusive,
Tauntin, "DUMB DOG YO -
I'LL bet you can't catch ME."
Challenged by that fish obtrusive
(I'll teach him to be abusive!)
I just snarled back,
"You're on! You can't match me."
Into icy waters dashing
Snorting, puffing, panting, splashing,
Oh I gave full chase with all my heart and soul.
My performance, keen and smashing,
Eyes and teeth in rhythm flashing,
But the "game was called!" -
HIS FISH WAS SWALLOWED WHOLE.

MICHAELMAS DAISIES

My Michaelmas daisies are blooming,
In cascades of purple and blue.
Bees buzzing away in the blossoms
Join in with fall's hullabaloo.
For autumn is nearly forgotten,
Her flowers becoming so few,
(And daisies too soon will be wearing
Not bees, but a snowflake or two.)

WITCHCRAFT IN CHESTER!

On one point Tom and "Yo" agree--
CHESTER DEALS IN SORCERY!
You have but to place one foot
On Plumas soil and it takes root.
So like a fresh cut willow twig
Out to really "make it big",
Thirsty roots proliferate
And suddenly it's just too late!
Chester has you in her spell,
CHARMED! You came, You saw, You fell!
LUCKY YOU!

FALL COTTONWOOD

Someone has pillaged
The vault at Fort Knox.
here's gold overflowing
For blocks and for blocks!
Yo kicks it, I scuff it
The wind makes a try
At setting it dancing
This gold from on high.
It's not legal tender
But still it will buy
The glories encompassed
Between Earth and sky.

WINTER IN CHESTER

A tiny house wrapped up in snow.
A mini-stove to brightly glow.
A snug retreat where thoughts may flow
And time to watch icicles grow!

SNOW CLOUDS

Bombarded by amorphous puffs
Of storm clouds ravaging, on high,
'Me sun, subdued to moon-stone-disk,
Found refuge in the pewter sky.

CHESTER
(October 1984)

Tempted by a catalogue
Whose blossoms challenged reason,
I sent a hefty order off,
Investment for next season.
Eagerly I waited as
Fall winds set trees a-quivering.
"Freeze tonight," the neighbor's said
All red of nose and shivering.
When at last my order came
'twas not with joy I smiled.
Where I had planned to plant my bulbs
SIX FOOT OF SNOW WAS PILED!
Suggestions?

S' NO FUN

Pine trees bedizened with winter's white wonder,
A saga of calm without equal.
Cascading snow that intrudes our snug mufflers
ordained, spine chilling sequel!

FOSSIL LEAF

A fragile bit impressed on stone
Forever free of age and clime.
Recorded life; a memory;
A leaf held in the hand of time.

YEAR'S END: 1985

December!
Silver sheets the silent meadow.
The earth lies foil to the moon's cold glow.
All being slumbers,
timed to winter's tempo.
Forever one with Chester,
so sleeps YO.

HEADED SOUTH!

Goodbye little house
with your ruffle of snow,
Your shiny green stove
and the fire's warm glow.
And bye little seeds,
just keep swelling and soon
We'll have a reunion –
It's not long 'til June!
Good bye little clock,
I have silenced your chime.
Come June,
and once more you can meter the time.
But now, join the sleepers,
and when it is Spring,
May your voice sound loudest
of all those that sing.

SHOW TIME IN CHESTER

The pussywillows waited in
The Tardy April snow,
All anxious for the opening of
THE WORLD'S GREATEST SHOW.
The Spring kissed earth; the Prompter cried
"We're on, all set, Let's go!"
A tarp, of emerald glistened and
The canopy was blue.
From far off a rainbow sent
Bright blossoms, right on cue
(But then the poppies claimed "the spot"
Each one an ingenue.)

Book Three -
Chester Vespers

CHRISTMAS CARD

God gives us life,
Life is for living.
God gives us love,
Love is forgiving.
(Christmas, 1993)

THOUGHTS IN CHURCH

FIRST THOUGHTS:
Dear God; I'm sitting here today
Because you've dragged me all the way.
I thundered "NO", you whispered "yes.'.'
But now I'm here, and will confess
It somehow feels so very "right', I wonder,
Has a robe of white been set aside for me?

AFTER THOUGHTS:

Dear God:
I'm kneeling here today
Because you've urged me all the way.
My stubborn "no" fell to your "yes"
I humbly yearn to acquiesce
Accepting all your grace can mete
But God, I still find apples sweet.

CORRECTION

The Bible assures us that apples
Caused Adam to tumble from Grace.
That is of course, only THEIR story
Let me tell you the truth of the case.
The tree was a native of Texas.
Pecans bowed the limbs
with their weight.

So naturally Eve munched
(and shared them)
This gift of the great Lone Star State;
They traded their fig leaves for Levis,
NO GARDEN! A ranch more their style.
They-beamed as they watched
their trees burgeon
They bask in the Texas sun and smile

It's FIE! to the serpent and apples,
And Eden is doing right well
Like Eve, I partake of its largeness
Like Adam, I'm pleased how things fell.
PARADISE!

VIEWPOINTS
AND CONCLUSIONS

The Bible tells us
"Man was made from dust."
"Ah no" said Darwin,
"Mankind has evolved."

A knotty problem for some few I guess,
But not for me!
THAT problem has been solved.
For instance, when I'm visiting a zoo
I have NO tendency to shout
"YOU HOOOOO."

But in a garden,
hunkered on my knees
I found soil,
rich with sentient might
I feel the heartbeat of my Mother Earth.

And am assured,
"The Bible tells it right."
Thanks Darwin for the scientific try,
Alas the tail you spin I cannot buy.

DAWN

Dawn floods over the rim of the world
Diffusing the mid-night blue.
The lagging stars disappear in the sky
At one with this day born new.

And I give thanks for the hours ahead
Well knowing God's rule applies,
NO DAY COMES FORTH
FROM THE MIND OF THE LORD
BEREFT OF A BLEST SURPRISE.

Dawn unfurled the perfect day
"Hands on care" is the rule of thumb.
Talisman of the perfect day,
Of all the days that are yet to come.

SHADOW SELF

I have a little shadow who's
Convinced that He is ME.
It's unbelievable how stubborn
That wee wraith can be.
He crashes into walls
Or slips in pools,
Or bumps his head,
And then he tries to tell me
I'm the bungler instead'!
Oh silly little shadow,
Who knows not wrong from right
It isn't hard to cope with you,
I just turn on the light!

PHILOSOPHY OF MISS JONES

ALMIGHTY GOD, UNCHALLENGED
As eons mist away
our light so much the clearer
Your law so much the dearer
Your love so much the nearer
NOW is that perfect day.
I was, I am, forever shall I be
Life-essence shuttling ceaselessly
Through life's God-plotted tapestry.
CONTINIUM
Though changing, still changeless,
Evolving, conforming to some endless
plan Emergence, erosion,
and sedimentation
These total the journals of earth and of men.
He sat at the foot of the golden stairs,
shrouded in Godless bloom,
To all who would climb to the heights above,
He grudgingly granted room.
But mumbled and muttered
"What fools these pilgrims be."
What do they think they will find above?
It's just a mirage they see.
BUT - There's a wind, a keening wind,
Repeating relentlessly
"I weep for one who having eyes,
is still reluctant to see."
Who can they mean, not me!

THE BIBLE RECYCLED:
DAVID vs GOLIATH

Goliath was a giant.
For thirty days and more
He terrorized an army.
Each day held stand and roar,
"Just send 'me out one soldier,
Some warrior that you prize,
And then stand by as witness,
I'LL CUT HIM DOWN TO SIZE!"

David was a shepherd,
A stalwart lad and true.
His weapons were a slingshot plus
What he with God could do.
The while Goliath blustered,
"Dave" shot him in the head.
One stone from David's sling shot,
GOLIATH FELL DOWN DEAD!

'Goliath was tall,
David was small
Who took the fall? GOLIATH!
Goliath had might.
David had-right.
Who lost the fight? GOLIATH!
Goliath cried THRUST!
David prayed TRUST
Who bit the dust? GOLIATH!

MRS. BECK

You've no doubt heard the tale as true
Of how God took the mist and the dew
And created the first man, named Adam,
But poor Adam alas was a bust
For he wailed "Please God, take my extra rib-bone
And make me a woman, I can't live alone!"

And no doubt you remember the serpent,
Eve fell for his wiles on sight,
And in falling dragged down poor old Ad
They tossed BOTH out of Eden that night. I
Oh how sad and how true that we suffer today
From actions of Eve - was there no other way?

Looking back on that day of creation
As viewed from today's modem tech
How much wiser had God not made Adam,
But instead had just made Mrs. Beck.

So efficient, so quick, there's no task past her skill
From chain saw to stove all things move at her will.
So with her as the first to be fashioned
Just no need for old Adam at all
Then all mankind could still live in Eden
With no cowering when God came to call
And the future of man, Mrs. Beck all ALONE?
Don't give it a thought; God has ways of his own!
(Besides which, there is nothing that woman cannot do,
if, she sets her mind to.

ONE BOON I ASK

One boon I ask,
That I may see MYSELF
As God HIMSELF sees me.

HE KEEPS MY EYES IN FOCUS

He keeps my eyes in focus.
My heart ticks right in time.
He modulates my breathing,
When there are stairs to climb.
I mirror my Creator,
I have no fear of glare
My God is my protector.
And God is everywhere.

Or is it REVELATION

I listened one night as I started to pray
And would you believe it? I heard myself say
"Now please pay attention God,
This is the way."

My prayers went unanswered,
And now I know why.
There was never a "you"
It was always an "I".

But now that I've listened,
And learned, I shall try
To follow submissively where You lead,
To be more alert to my fellow-man's need,
Be loving and grateful,
to serve and to cede-
To You all decisions
that once I made mine
Adhering permissively to this new line
I soon shall imbibe of Celestial wine....
(Most docile of all angels that have ever
Flown over the Gates of Paradise!)

SHE TURNED TO GOD

She turned to God for succor.
Most humbly she pleaded,
"PLEASE GIVE ME STRENGTH!"
Her answer -
Ten times the strength she needed.

And with the added muscle
Her burdens grew much greater.
NO DOUBT MY PRAYER WAS ANSWERED –
BUT - We heard her mutter later ....
NEXT TIME I'LL JUST QUOTE SCRIPTURE
"THY WILL BE DONE,"
SHOULD DO IT.
WHEN I ASK SPECIAL FAVORS
I GET THEM,
BUT I RUE IT.

NEED A LIFT?

When you find your spirit sagging
And your weary tail dragging
That's not the time to stop and pamper
That's the time to help another.
Clasp his hand and call him Brother,
Come on! Step up!
There's nothing hindering you.
Then you'll find you've turned jolly,
All entwined with Christmas Holly,
The woeful you is now a happy sprite.
Although it's still a mystery
It's been known all through history
When you help Him,
it's you that sees the light!

MICROCOSM vs. MACROCOSM

Mind, little mind,
Kindly quell your delusions,
Your spurious reasoning
Evolves false conclusions.

Mind, little mind,
It's not YOU that's clever,
Pay homage; acknowledge;
But claim credit?
NEVER!

You are a phony!
Just no need to chortle,
Your flashy techniques
Will not crash heaven's portal.

Face up little mind,
You're just NOT a creator!
So wheel and deal and seek your niche.

I'm sure you will know
when you're locked into place.
(And we'll know it too,
for there's certain to be
a smile of triumph adoring your face!)

THE MOUNTAIN IS THERE
FOR CLIMBING

The mountain's there for climbing
The summit still a mystery
Perhaps it's time to heed
The hinted word of History,
LOVE THY NEIGHBOR

As I ascend the narrow way
Life and Love companion me.
Three in one--God's Trinity
So it is that one, not three
Shall probe into eternity.

The wise man is good
And the good man is wise
He listens to God and Obeys.

He welcomes corrections
Gives heed to directions
And glorifies God all his days.

A FINAL WORD FROM CLEIL...

Upon Cleil's passing, I received this letter
from her son, Robert:

March 23, 1999
Dear Lori,

"Thank you very much for your card.
The service was held in Chester which pulled out all the stops
and provided us with an incredible snow storm.
Thus Chester was dressed up in its best
in order to say goodbye.
The snow ended with the very simple service
which was mostly attended by family
and a few friends who lived in Chester.
Cleil did not want a funeral
and had asked many of her closest friends to stay away.
After the service, Teen Van V read one of Cleil's poems:

Now I lay me down to die
My face upturned to search the sky
As I have been so shall I be
A fragment of Eternity.

A two pound box of See's Candy allowed people to take a
communion that Cleil would have understood best.
We gave those who attended books of Cleil's poems.
Sincerely,
Robert Turkington"

Cleil Turkington's Kids – Mike, Mickey, Robert, Tom

NAME INDEX

More Books from ACCESS PRESS on Amazon

ADOPT-A-QUOTE
400 Inspirational Quotes, Slogans & Poems By and For Those Touched by Adoption

THE ULTIMATE SEARCH BOOK – U.S & World Editions
(U.S. Adoption, Genealogy & Other Search Secrets)

CHOSEN CHILDREN
(People, Politics and America's Failed Foster Care and Adoption Industries)

ADOPTION UNCENSORED *(4 Decades of Politics, People and Commentary)*

THE ADOPTION AND DONOR CONCEPTION FACTBOOK
*(The Only Comprehensive Source of U.S. & Global Data
On the Invisible Families of Adoption, Foster Care & Donor Conception)*

BLOOD RELATIVES *(A True Story of Family Secrets & Murders)*

SERIAL KILLERS ON THE INTERSTATE
(100 Highway Killers by State)

KILLERS ONLINE *(100 True Stories)*

KONDRO *(The "Uncle Joe" Killer)*

ESPOSITO *(The First Mafioso)*

PAST MISTAKES *(Is Joe Garcia the Central Coast Rapist?)*

FRAMED! *(The Carefully Crafted Central Coast Rapist)*

RAGE! *(How An Adoption Ignited a Fire)*

ADOPTED KILLERS *(430 Adoptees Who Killed – How and Why They Did It)*

8 BALL CAFÉ *(Stories of Adoption, Addiction and Redemption)*

FROM ITALIAN-AMERICA WITH LOVE *(Cookbook)*
FROM ITALY & ITALIANS OF ALL NATIONS WITH LOVE *(Cookbook)*

www.ingramcontent.com/pod-product-compliance
Lightning Source LLC
Chambersburg PA
CBHW050132280326
41933CB00010B/1349